DRAMATIC HOURS
IN REVOLUTIONARY HISTORY

Washington
Crossing the Delaware

BY

HENRY FISK CARLTON

Edited by CLAIRE T. ZYVE, PH.D.
Fox Meadow School, Scarsdale, New York

HOW TO BE A GOOD RADIO ACTOR

The play in this book has actually been produced on the radio. Possibly you have listened to this one when you tuned in at home. The persons whose voices you heard as you listened, looked just as they did when they left their homes to go to the studio, although they were taking the parts of men and women who lived long ago and who wore costumes very different from the ones we wear today.

The persons whose voices you heard stood close together around the microphone, each one reading from a copy of the play in his hand. Since they could not be seen, they did not act parts as in other plays, but tried to make their voices show how they felt.

When you give these plays you will not need costumes and you will not need scenery, although you can easily arrange a broadcasting studio if you wish. You will not need to memorize your parts; in fact, it will not be like a real radio broadcast if you do so, and, furthermore, you will not want to, since you will each have a copy of the book in your hands. All you will need to do is to remember that you are taking the part of a radio actor, that you are to read your speeches very distinctly, and that by your voice you will make your audience understand how you feel. In this way you will have the fun of living through some of the great moments of history.

HOW TO FOLLOW DIRECTIONS
IN THE PLAY

There are some directions in this play which may be new to you, but these are necessary, for you are now in a radio broadcasting studio, talking in front of a microphone. The word (*in*) means that the character is standing close to the microphone, while (*off*) indicates that he is farther away, so that his voice sounds faint. When the directions (*off, coming in*) are given, the person speaking is away from the microphone at first but gradually comes closer. The words (*mob*) or (*crowd noise*) you will understand mean the sound of many people talking in the distance.

Both the English and the dialect used help make the characters live, so the speeches have been written in the way in which these men and women would talk. This means that sometimes the character may use what seems to you unusual English. The punctuation helps, too, to make the speeches sound like real conversation; for example, you will find that a dash is often used to show that a character is talking very excitedly.

WASHINGTON CROSSING THE DELAWARE

CAST

GENERAL WASHINGTON
COLONEL REED
JOHN HONEYMAN
COLONEL RALL
A CORPORAL
A SOLDIER
GENERAL KNOX
COLONEL GLOVER
MOB
VOICE
ORDERLY

ANNOUNCER

We take pleasure in presenting this story of Washington crossing the Delaware. The picture of that famous event is familiar to everyone, but the story of what led up to it, and of its importance in American history is not so well known.

The fall and early winter of the year 1776 saw the fortunes of Washington's army sink very low indeed. Beginning with the defeat on Long Island in late August, Washington and his army had met reverse after reverse. They had been forced to retire in succession from Manhattan to Fort Washington, then across the river to Fort Lee, then from Fort Lee to Hackensack. This succession of defeats and the enforced retirements had disorganized and depleted the army. But even worse than that, it had well-nigh ruined the morale of the civilian population, whose hearty support was absolutely necessary if the war was to be carried on. But now, discouraged and disheartened, the mass of the population gave Washington no help, no encouragement, no cooperation.

This is the situation on the morning of November 22, 1776, as we begin our story. Washington is in his headquarters at Hackensack, New Jersey, when Colonel Joseph Reed, his aide, enters—

REED

Good morning, General Washington!

WASHINGTON

Good morning, Colonel, what news?

REED

Not much, I'm afraid, sir.

WASHINGTON

Have we no information of the British movements yet?

REED

None!

WASHINGTON

What's the matter with our intelligence service?

REED

It's completely disrupted, sir; and we can get no help from the civilian population.

WASHINGTON

I know—they've lost all faith in us, Colonel. Nothing but a victory can bring us again the loyalty and help of our own people! It's discouraging, Colonel, to think that now when we need it more than ever before, we can get no help!

REED

Sir, if we could only turn and strike a quick blow, we might recapture Fort Lee.

WASHINGTON

Yes—if I only knew what force of the enemy is holding the Fort, and when Lord Howe expects to bring the rest of his army across the Hudson.

REED

Well, we don't know that!

WASHINGTON

And without an intelligence service we can't find out! Of course if General Lee would join me—there wasn't any word from Lee this morning, was there?

REED

None, sir.

WASHINGTON

Oh, why doesn't he answer? Why doesn't he come? It's been more than a week now since I ordered him to join me at once! Have you heard any rumor about him? Has he left Peekskill yet? Has he crossed the Hudson?

REED

I haven't heard a word. He hasn't even acknowledged the last half dozen orders I've forwarded to him.

WASHINGTON

That's the most discouraging thing of all! If the second in command won't obey orders, is it any wonder that the rest of the army is out of hand? Oh, well! We can't hope to do anything without Lee's help, so there's nothing for us to do but retreat—

REED

Again?

WASHINGTON

Yes, Colonel, our small force is uselessly exposed here. We can't risk capture—that would be the end of everything!

REED

Yes, sir.

WASHINGTON

If Lord Howe crosses the Hudson in force, we'd be trapped between the Hackensack and the Passaic Rivers.

REED

I'm afraid so, sir.

WASHINGTON

So—we've got to begin our retreat at once.

REED

The troops are ready to move, sir. It shouldn't take us long to get out of danger with our small force.

WASHINGTON

Yes, yes, that's one advantage of a small army, isn't it, Colonel? At least we can retreat rapidly! I suppose the force we have is even smaller today than it was yesterday?

REED

I'm afraid so, sir. The morning report showed less than five thousand present and fit for duty!

WASHINGTON

If we only had Lee's seven thousand! But we haven't. You may order the retreat at once, Colonel.

REED

Yes sir, over what route?

WASHINGTON

We'll move across the Acquackonack bridge, and thence to Newark.

REED

Yes, sir. I'll write the orders, sir. (*rattle of paper*)

WASHINGTON

Colonel John Glover with his Marblehead regiment will cover the retreat as usual.

REED

Yes, sir. And the advance?

WASHINGTON

Knox and his artillery will lead. We mustn't lose our guns—the few we have left.

REED

Yes, sir.

WASHINGTON (half to himself)

Retreat—retreat—retreat! Is there nothing else in store for us?

REED

Will you sign these, sir?

WASHINGTON

Yes—the quill.

REED

Here you are, sir.

WASHINGTON

Thank you. (*rattle of paper*) You may send the orders at once, Colonel.

REED

Yes, General. (*calling*) Orderly!

VOICE

Yes, sir.

REED

Deliver these orders at once!

VOICE

Yes, sir.

WASHINGTON

I suppose it's useless to send another order to Lee.

REED

We can send one—I don't think it will have any effect.

WASHINGTON

He ought to be informed of where we're going— yes, write him again, tell him we're retreating to Newark—

REED

Very well, sir—and after Newark?

WASHINGTON

Retreat again I suppose. New Brunswick— Trenton—across the Delaware into Pennsylvania.

REED

Yes sir, if we have any army left by then.

WASHINGTON

We have some loyal souls who will stand with us to the end. We may have to retreat to the back country of Pennsylvania; but winter is coming, Lord Howe is not an energetic foe, and he will hardly press us after the snow falls. Then if we can fill up our depleted ranks we'll be ready for him in the spring.

REED

Oh, General, if we could only make one stand against the enemy! Make one bold stroke to put new heart into our discouraged countrymen!

WASHINGTON

I know—I know, Colonel! If Lee would only obey my orders!

REED

Very little hope of that!

WASHINGTON

I know—and I can't understand his motives!

REED

Why sir, they're perfectly plain to me—and to the rest of the army.

WASHINGTON

Indeed?

REED

Certainly—he wants to discredit you—to bring about your failure—so that he can succeed to your command!

WASHINGTON

So—? (*pause*) Well, if Lee can bring victory where I have failed, I'll be only too glad to step down in his favor.

REED

Sir, I beg of you, you mustn't even entertain such a thought, why General Lee could no more—(*knock*)

WASHINGTON

Will you see who it is, Colonel.

REED

Yes, sir—(*mumble at a distance, then out loud*) General, there's a man here who wants to see you.

WASHINGTON

Who is it?

REED

He refuses to give his name, and says his business is private.

WASHINGTON

Tell him to come in.

REED

Yes, sir—(*off*) Come on in, the General will see you.

HONEYMAN

Thankee—thankee, sir. I'm obleeged to ye, sir. (*in*) Be ye General Washington?

WASHINGTON

I am, and what can I do for you?

HONEYMAN

Wal'—General—if ye don't mind—er—er—

WASHINGTON

Yes?

HONEYMAN

I'd like to see ye alone—sir—it's important!

WASHINGTON

Alone? Oh, very well, Colonel—

REED

I'll go, sir.

WASHINGTON

Write that letter to Lee.

REED (*going*)

Yes, sir. (*door closes*)

WASHINGTON

Now, what is it?

HONEYMAN

Wal', here I be, General—

WASHINGTON

Yes?

HONEYMAN

An' I've had tarnation's own time gittin' here—I cal'ate half yer army stopped me an' wanted to know my name an' my business—an' they wasn't goin' to let me in when I wouldn't tell 'em. But it takes more'n that to stop John Honeyman when he gits sot on doin' something.

WASHINGTON

Your name is John Honeyman?

HONEYMAN

That's me, sir, an' I promised Marthy—that's my wife, sir—that I'd come to see ye—and I come, an' here I be!

WASHINGTON

And what can I do for you, Mr. Honeyman?

HONEYMAN

Nary a thing, General Washington.

WASHINGTON

Then what—?

HONEYMAN

I come to make ye an offer.

WASHINGTON

Well?

HONEYMAN

I'm in a way to find out a lot o' things that's goin' on in the British Army.

WASHINGTON

So?

HONEYMAN

Aye, ye see, I'm a butcher.

WASHINGTON

Well?

HONEYMAN

An' I've got a contract to supply the redcoats with beef. Now they think I'm a good Tory! But General, I ain't!

WASHINGTON

I'm glad to hear that!

HONEYMAN

An' I figgered that mebbe I could find out things an' tell ye about 'em—if we could fix things up.

WASHINGTON

How much do you want for your information?

HONEYMAN

No! No! General! I ain't tryin' to sell ye nothin'!

WASHINGTON

I beg your pardon, Mr. Honeyman. But I have so many insincere offers.

HONEYMAN

I know—I know! I hear folks talk. They think I'm a Tory! Wal', sir, I want they should keep on a-thinkin' it! I cal'ate if I'm a-goin' to be any use to ye, nobody must know I ain't a rip-roarin' all-fired Tory.

WASHINGTON

Certainly!

HONEYMAN

An' that's the why I wouldn't tell none o' yer men what my name er my business was.

WASHINGTON

Mr. Honeyman, you've shown extraordinary good sense! You're exactly the man I've been looking for! I'm in desperate need of reliable information. And I believe you're the man to get it for me.

HONEYMAN

I cal'ate I be.

WASHINGTON

Have you any information now?

HONEYMAN

A mite.

WASHINGTON

Well?

HONEYMAN

Lord Cornwallis is bringin' 15,000 men across the Hudson tonight, to git ye.

WASHINGTON

We'll be gone.

HONEYMAN

That's fu'st-rate! Now I'll be goin'—an' I'll keep ye informed when I know anything ye ought to know.

WASHINGTON

Just a moment, Honeyman. How are you going to get your information to me?

HONEYMAN

Wal', I figger I might come to see ye—

WASHINGTON

No, you'd be sure to excite suspicion.

HONEYMAN

I'd be as keerful as could be.

WASHINGTON

No—I mustn't even let my own men know you're working for me.

HONEYMAN

Wal'—ye might have me captured now an' agin—
tell yer men I'm a notorious Tory—an' have 'em be
on the lookout fer me particular! Then when I've got
something fer ye, I'll put myself in the way o' gittin'
captured.

WASHINGTON

Good! That's an excellent idea. I'll have to give you
a pretty bad name with my troops.

HONEYMAN

Pshaw—I don't mind that, sir.

WASHINGTON

And I don't know how I can reward you.

HONEYMAN

I don't need no reward to help ye, General
Washington, I got a duty to do that!—There's only
jest one thing, sir—

WASHINGTON

Yes?

HONEYMAN

I'd sorta—er—kinda like my wife an' children protected from the—wal'—the results o' my bein' an active an' notorious Tory.

WASHINGTON

Of course.

HONEYMAN

Ye see, I don't mind what folks think o' me, but Marthy—that's my wife, sir—she an' the young un's might git—wal'—treated pretty shabby.

WASHINGTON

I understand. I'll give you an order for them to use in case of necessity.

HONEYMAN

Would ye—er—sign it yerself, General?

WASHINGTON

Certainly! Here—I'll write it now. (*rattle of paper*) Let's see—(*slowly*) "To the Good People of New Jersey and all others it may concern: It is ordered that the wife and children of John Honeyman of—" Where's your home?

HONEYMAN

Grigstown, sir.

WASHINGTON

"—of Grigstown, the notorious Tory now within the British lines and probably acting the part of a British spy, should be protected from all harm and annoyances. This is no protection to Honeyman himself." Is that satisfactory?

HONEYMAN

I cal'ate that covers it, sir.

WASHINGTON

Very well, I'll sign it—(*signing*) There you are, sir.

HONEYMAN

I'm much obleeged to ye, sir.

WASHINGTON

No, Honeyman, I'm the one who is your debtor. Good day, sir.

HONEYMAN

Good day, General Washington. Next time ye see me I'll be yer prisoner.

ANNOUNCER

And John Honeyman left Washington's camp to set about making his position secure with the British. He became one of the regular meat contractors for Cornwallis's army, which pursued Washington across the state of New Jersey during the next month.

Washington did not hurry his retreat, but he always got away. Finally about the first of December, he came to Trenton, where he halted for a week and sent men up and down the river to collect all the boats on the Delaware. He knew that he would be forced to retreat into Pennsylvania; and he proposed to leave no means for the enemy to follow him. On December 8, 1776, the British advance, which consisted of a brigade of Hessians under Colonel Rall, entered Trenton; but as usual, Washington was half a day ahead of his pursuers, and as the Hessians entered the village, the rear guard of the Americans was just entering the last of the boats, and safely pulled away to the Pennsylvania shore! Lord Howe, who had joined Cornwallis, sent out men to look for boats, but none could be found. The weather turned cold. Lord Howe was uncomfortable; so he decided to put his troops into winter quarters and let the pursuit go. He had done enough for one season!

He and Cornwallis arranged to scatter the troops about New Jersey to hold that territory, while they went back to New York to enjoy the winter.

Trenton was left in charge of Colonel Rall and his brigade of Hessians. On December 22, John Honeyman drove a small herd of cattle into Trenton, left them standing in front of headquarters, as he went up and knocked on the door. (*knocks*)

RALL (*off*)

Come in! Come in!

HONEYMAN

Mornin', Colonel Rall!

RALL

Oh, it's you, Honeyman!

HONEYMAN

Aye, it's me—an' I got some cattle out front here fer yer Quartermaster.

RALL

Well, that's good news—my men will be glad to see that beef! Now we can give 'em a Christmas dinner that'll *be* a Christmas dinner!

HONEYMAN

All ye need now, Colonel, is a mite o' wine, eh?

RALL

Never fear, we've got the wine!

HONEYMAN

Wal', ye kin have a fu'st-rate Christmas then.

RALL

Yes sir! With roast beef and two hogsheads of fine wine—we should do very well.

HONEYMAN

Two? Pshaw, is that all?

RALL

Why—what's the matter with that?

HONEYMAN

Two hogsheads won't go so far with a whole brigade.

RALL

Oh, I haven't got a whole brigade.

HONEYMAN

Ye ain't?

RALL

No, just a thousand men, that's all! Why sir, they can all get roarin' drunk on the ration I'll issue 'em.

HONEYMAN

An' like as not they will, eh, Colonel?

RALL (chuckling)

Well, Honeyman, what do you expect o' soldiers? Christmas you know—and out here in this God-forsaken place. Let 'em get drunk, I say. There's nothing else to do.

HONEYMAN

Wal', Colonel, I cal'ate 'tain't often ye find a better officer than ye be! I'd like to serve under ye!

RALL

Well, if you want—

HONEYMAN

Yes, sir. I'd do it if I wasn't helpin' along things in my way by roundin' up food fer the king's men. Wal', mebbe ye better sign fer these critters out in front an' I'll be gittin' along. I got to hike over to the next post. Er—by the way—how fer is it to the next detachment o' troops?

RALL

Oh, about six miles south.

HONEYMAN

Six miles, huh? How fer to the next one north?

RALL

Nobody north of us.

HONEYMAN

Eh, nobody north?

RALL

No, I'm command of the flank. This is the last post.

HONEYMAN

I cal'ate that makes a lot o' hard work fer ye, Colonel?

RALL

Hard work?

HONEYMAN

Sure, don't ye have to patrol up an' down the river, an' sich like things?

RALL (laughing)

What for?

HONEYMAN

Wal', after all, there's *some* o' the enemy left, ain't there?

RALL (laughing)

A half-a-dozen starved ragamuffins. What could they do to my trained Hessians?

HONEYMAN (joining in the laugh)

Not much, I cal'ate! Ye ain't in much danger, an' that's a fact!

RALL

If we had some boats we'd soon make short work of them. But confound the rascals, they made away with all the boats.

HONEYMAN

Ye ain't got no boats, eh?

RALL

Not a one!

HONEYMAN

Ye ain't built none, eh?

RALL

Why should we?

HONEYMAN

Wal'—if ye want to git across the river—

RALL

Oh, we'll get across as soon as the river freezes over. We'll get the last o' the rebels then.

HONEYMAN

Wal', Colonel, good luck to ye. But I hope ye won't be in too big a hurry to capture all the rebels!

RALL

Eh, what's that?

HONEYMAN

Er—I'll be out of a job; and so'll ye be, Colonel!

RALL

Yes, that's right too. Well, let's have a look at your cattle and I'll sign for 'em.

HONEYMAN

Come on—you fu'st, sir.

RALL

Thanks—hm—how many did you say there were?

HONEYMAN

There's twenty-two critters there—er, there was when I drove 'em up.

RALL

Hm—they look a little scrawny.

HONEYMAN

Best I could git, Colonel!

RALL (counting)

Two—four—five—seven—ten (*etc.*) Hm—twenty-one's all I make, Honeyman.

HONEYMAN

Twenty-one? Pshaw now—did one o' them critters go trapsin' off. (*he counts*) Yes sir, that's just what's happened. Wall—sign fer the twenty-one, an' I'll go out lookin' fer that other critter.

RALL

Here you are—let me have that bill—(*rattle of paper*) Twenty-one in good condition, signed— Rall. There you are. Hope you find the other one.

HONEYMAN

Thankee—where's that road off to the left go?

RALL

That—oh, that's the river road.

HONEYMAN

I cal'ate the critter musta gone that way.

RALL

Better keep a sharp lookout if you go down that way.

HONEYMAN

Eh? What fer?

RALL

Some o' those ragamuffin rebels might be on this side of the river.

HONEYMAN

Pshaw now—ye don't say! They come across the river, do they?

RALL

Yes, once in a while. But they don't dare bother us. But they might pick up a civilian.

HONEYMAN

Oh, I cal'ate I kin take keer o' myself. I got my whip and this halter.

RALL (laughing)

That ought to be enough to scare 'em away from you!

HONEYMAN (*going*)

They'll figger I'm the hangman come out to git 'em—fetchin' my halter along! (*he and* RALL *laugh*)

ANNOUNCER

So Honeyman started down the river road, cracking his whip and swinging his halter. A couple of miles down the road, four Continental soldiers were in hiding. They had been sent out with instructions to pick up a prisoner, if possible, and bring him into Washington's headquarters for the purpose of securing information. As Honeyman drew near their place of hiding in the brush alongside the river road, the men heard the snapping of his whip. (*crack of whip*)

CORPORAL (*low*)

What's that?

SOLDIER

Don't know, sounds funny. See anything, Corporal?

CORPORAL

There, I see him! Huh, it's just a farmer crackin' his driving whip.

SOLDIER

Yah, I see him. What's he got in his other hand?

CORPORAL

Looks like a piece o' rope.

SOLDIER

A halter! Look, Corporal!

CORPORAL

Yep. A halter. Well, no use stoppin' him. Lie low. We want to get one o' them Hessians. By George, though, I'd like to have that whip.

SOLDIER

What for?

CORPORAL

To use on the Hessians we're goin' to git!

SOLDIER

You bet. Them mercenaries ought to be whipped out o' the country! Shootin's too good for 'em—we'd ought to—

CORPORAL

Sh! He's gettin' closer.

SOLDIER

Say! I know that fellow.

CORPORAL

Yah? What about it? Keep quiet, I said!

SOLDIER

No! Listen, Corporal, we got to capture him.

CORPORAL

Why?

SOLDIER

The General issued orders about him.

CORPORAL

Who is he?

SOLDIER

Honeyman!

CORPORAL

Honeyman the Tory?

SOLDIER

That's who it is. Let's grab him.

CORPORAL

Men! (*several voices respond*) We're going to take this fellow. All right now—lie low—and when I give the signal, jump!

HONEYMAN (off, coming in)

So-o-o, boss—where's that dang critter gone to? I cal'ate mebbe—

CORPORAL

Halt! Get him boys!

HONEYMAN

Say! What's the matter—what ye doin'!

ALL

Come on! Grab him! Get hold of him there! Down with him! (*etc.*)

HONEYMAN (at same time)

Hey, you scoundrels! Git off me! Leave me be! I'm a peaceable man, ye ain't got no right to do this to me—git off me—git off—I say—hey, leave go my halter!

SOLDIERS

Well, ain't this nice, boys. He's brought along a rope for us to tie him up with, now ain't that thoughtful—here—leave go the rope.

HONEYMAN

Let me up—don't ye tie me up! I'm jest a farmer—out huntin' a stray cow!

CORPORAL

Stray cow, eh? Well, we was huntin' a stray coward! (*laughter*) Here give me that whip!

SOLDIER

Here ye are, Corporal! Well boys, take a look at him—this here's Honeyman the Tory. (*all comment*)

CORPORAL

All right, throw him into the boat! General Washington'll be right pleased to see ye, Mister Honeyman! Come along—oh, ye won't go, eh—well, fetch him, boys.

HONEYMAN

Leave me be! Stop it! The King's men'll make ye pay fer this.

ALL

Hey shut up—grab him Tom—stop that kickin', fetch him along. (*etc.*)

ANNOUNCER

Protesting and struggling, Honeyman was thrown into the boat and carried to the Pennsylvania shore of the Delaware. In the meantime, on that very afternoon of December 22, 1776, Washington was holding a council of war with his staff.

WASHINGTON

Gentlemen, I regret to inform you that Congress has fled from Philadelphia.

ALL

What? Fled? Left Philadelphia? Too bad! (*etc.*)

WASHINGTON

I'm sorry! I asked them particularly to stay there, as I feared the effect on the people of the country. But it seems that even Congress has lost faith in the army.

KNOX

General Washington.

WASHINGTON

General Knox.

KNOX

We've got to do something to re-establish their faith! (*all agree*)

WASHINGTON

Yes! But what? Charles Lee is captured—his army gone—we can't look for any help from that quarter.

KNOX

Sir, can't we go back across the river, suddenly—and strike a blow before the enemy knows what we are up to?

WASHINGTON

We'll have to! It's our only hope. But how, when, and where? I had hoped that we might get information that would guide us in our plans. Well, we haven't got it! Now, much as I hate to make any move without full and complete information, I don't see what else we can do. The river will be frozen over in a week or ten days. That means that the enemy can cross over and chase us whither they please! If we are to do anything, we've got to do it now! I've called you here to lay this before you. Will you follow me on a blind chance?

ALL

Yes! We will! You can count on us, sir. (*etc.*)

WASHINGTON

I want you all to realize that this is a desperate chance. Failure means—well, we might as well face it—it means the end of our cause; but success— well, gentlemen, we can only hope and pray for success! (*knock*) Will you see who's at the door, Colonel Reed?

REED

Yes, sir.

WASHINGTON

Tell whoever it is to come back later—I'm in council.

REED

Yes, sir. (*a mumble at the door*) I beg pardon, sir, they've just brought in a prisoner.

WASHINGTON

Good, tell them to wait outside.

REED

They say, sir, it's Honeyman the Tory, and you left orders—

WASHINGTON

Honeyman? Excellent! Gentlemen, I must ask you to leave me.

ALL

Yes sir, General, of course. (*etc.*)

WASHINGTON

You may hold yourselves in readiness for action. I'll issue the orders shortly.

ALL (*going*)

Yes, sir. Very good, sir. (*etc.*)

WASHINGTON

Bring the prisoner in, Colonel Reed.

REED (*off*)

Yes, sir. Bring him in, men.

VOICES (*coming in*)

Here you are—come along. (*etc.*)

CORPORAL

Here he is, General, that Tory you wanted, sir.

WASHINGTON

Very good, men. You may go.

CORPORAL

Can you handle him safe, sir?

WASHINGTON

He seems to be well bound. I think I'll have no trouble.

CORPORAL

Yes, sir. Very good, sir. Come on, men. We'll wait outside, sir.

WASHINGTON (*loud*)

Well, Honeyman. We've got you at last, eh?

HONEYMAN (*loud*)

I demand to be set free. Ye'll all answer to yer King fer this. (*door shuts*)

WASHINGTON (*low*)

What news?

HONEYMAN

Across the river in Trenton there ain't but a thousand Hessians.

WASHINGTON

Who's commanding?

HONEYMAN

Colonel Rall, and he ain't none too keerful—no patrols up er down the river—nobody at all north of him, and six miles to the nearest post on the south of him.

WASHINGTON

Excellent—excellent! We can do it! I'll order the attack tomorrow night! We'll trap them! We'll fight for once instead of retreat—we'll—

HONEYMAN

Beggin' yer pardon, sir.

WASHINGTON

Well?

HONEYMAN

If yer figgerin' on attackin', the time is Christmas night!

WASHINGTON

Why?

HONEYMAN

On Christmas the Hessians are goin' to git a big issue o' heavy wine, an' wal'—General—ye know soldiers—I don't have to say no more!

WASHINGTON

Good! Christmas night! Yes that's it! Has Colonel Rall taken any precautions against surprise?

HONEYMAN

Nary a one that I could see. He ain't a mite o' use fer you er yer soldiers. Ragamuffins he called 'em.

WASHINGTON

Ragamuffins? Yes, they are, poor fellows, but Honeyman, we'll see—perhaps ragamuffins can fight when they're given the chance—and with this information, you have given us our chance!

HONEYMAN

Wal', sir, I thought ye'd like to know.

WASHINGTON

Now, shall I turn you lose, Honeyman?

HONEYMAN

No, General, I figger ye'd better treat me like a prisoner er I can't be any more use to ye.

WASHINGTON

True, very well then. I'll have you put in the guardhouse and contrive to have you escape.

HONEYMAN

Yes, sir.

WASHINGTON (*calling*)

Oh, Orderly!

VOICE (*off*)

Yes, sir.

WASHINGTON

Tell the Corporal who's waiting out there to come in and take his prisoner to the guardhouse.

ORDERLY

Yes, sir—Corporal, come take charge of your prisoner.

CORPORAL (off, coming in)

Come on, men! Fall in around the prisoner—and look sharp that he doesn't try anything—forward march! (*sound of feet receding*)

WASHINGTON (*to himself*)

Christmas night! Trenton—God be with us!

ANNOUNCER

That night, by some unexplained accident, John Honeyman escaped from the guardhouse and returned to the British lines, where he continued his valuable service for the American cause.

Washington, with the information that Honeyman had brought him, was able to lay his plans intelligently and carefully.

Just after dusk has fallen on Christmas night, Washington orders his troops to the shore of the river. Snow is falling and the wind is howling, as Washington and Knox stand together near the boat landing—(*wind and murmur of crowd with occasional sharp commands in background through this scene.*)

WASHINGTON

This weather ought to help us, Knox.

KNOX

Brrr—it's cold enough to keep the Hessians indoors—if that's what you mean, General.

WASHINGTON

The snow will cover our movements.

KNOX

Yes—in more ways than one, General.

VOICE (*off*)

First brigade is formed, sir.

WASHINGTON

Very good. (*lower*) Order embarkation to begin, Knox.

KNOX

Artillery first, sir?

WASHINGTON

No, a company of foot soldiers first to stand guard and protect the landing.

KNOX

Yes, sir. (*calling*) General Green!

VOICE (*off*)

Yes, sir.

KNOX

Send one of your companies across first to stand guard and protect the landing.

VOICE

Very good, sir. Company A, into the boats! (*orders and mob confusion*)

KNOX

The river looks bad, sir. See all the ice? It looks wicked!

WASHINGTON

Ice! Hm—I hadn't foreseen this.

VOICE (*calling*)

General Knox!

KNOX

What is it?

VOICE

The boatmen say they can't make it, sir.

WASHINGTON

Can't make it? But they've got to!

VOICE

Sorry sir, they say the floating ice—

WASHINGTON

Call Colonel Glover, Knox!

KNOX (*calling*)

Glover! Colonel Glover! Pass the word for Colonel Glover. (*order repeated several times at different distances*)

WASHINGTON

We've got to get across, Knox, we've got to! If this attempt fails, there's nothing left for us! Nothing!

KNOX

We'll get across, sir, if we have to swim.

GLOVER (*coming in*)

Colonel Glover reports, sir.

WASHINGTON

Colonel Glover, can your regiment of seafaring men handle our boats in that river?

GLOVER

General Washington, my men can handle boats in any water!

WASHINGTON

The boatmen say they can't cross because of the floating ice.

GLOVER

Sir, my men are *sea* sailors, not river boatmen—it takes more than ice to scare them off!

WASHINGTON

Good! Put some of them in every boat.

GLOVER

Yes, sir.

WASHINGTON

And you will take general charge of the entire fleet.

GLOVER

Very good, sir.

WASHINGTON

Tell them to listen to General Knox's commands. He is the only one whose voice can be heard in this storm!

GLOVER

Very good, sir! (*going out*) This way, the Marblehead regiment! This way to the boats! (*mob*)

ANNOUNCER

For the next nine hours the difficult work of crossing the ice-filled river went forward. Colonel Glover and his regiment of seafaring men from Marblehead, Massachusetts, performed almost miraculous service in landing every man, horse, and gun without losing anything!

It was five o'clock in the morning of December 26 when Washington, now on the Jersey shore of the river, turned to Knox—(*wind and crowd noise*)

WASHINGTON

Has the last boatload landed, Knox?

KNOX

Yes, sir.

WASHINGTON

Call the men to attention.

KNOX (*calling*)

Call your men to attention!

VOICES

Company—company! (*etc.*) Attention! First regiment is formed, sir, second—(*etc.*)

KNOX

The men are formed, sir.

WASHINGTON

Men, we are about to start upon our most important offensive. Upon the results of our efforts this morning depends the outcome of our struggle for liberty and independence.

I shall take the first brigade and half the artillery with me down the Pennington road. The rest of the detachment under command of General Green will take the river road. It should take us about four hours to reach the outposts of Trenton. Now, it is necessary for us to attack simultaneously, so will the officers all set their watches with mine. It is now just five o'clock and ten minutes. At nine o'clock, attack!

Let every man march quietly, keep in good order in the ranks, give prompt obedience to his officers, and bear in mind the watchword—*Victory or Death!* March your men off!

VOICES

First Regiment—Second Regiment—Company—Company—(*etc.*)

ANNOUNCER

Thus, on that cold and stormy December morning, the half frozen, desperate band of ragamuffin soldiers started its march toward Trenton—toward its last forlorn hope. Washington prayed that he might catch the garrison of Hessians unsuspecting and unprepared; but he feared that he had taken so long to effect the crossing of the ice-filled river that he could not surprise the enemy!

As a matter of fact, warning was sent to Colonel Rall, but that officer, secure in his belief that no effective force of Colonial soldiers could be sent against him, paid no attention to the warning.

It was nearly nine o'clock when the Corporal of the advance guard of Washington's detachment hurried back to report to the General.

CORPORAL

General Washington, we've sighted the enemy outpost.

WASHINGTON

Good! Halt the brigade, Knox.

KNOX

Brigade!

VOICES

Company—company! (*etc.*)

KNOX

Halt!

WASHINGTON

It lacks five minutes of the time set! Oh, Corporal—

CORPORAL

Yes, sir?

WASHINGTON

Did you see any sign of General Green's command on the river road?

CORPORAL

We saw 'em a half hour ago, sir, as we came over that hill back there.

WASHINGTON

Were they abreast of us?

CORPORAL

Yes, sir, a little ahead of us, sir.

WASHINGTON

Good. General Knox.

KNOX

Yes, sir.

WASHINGTON

This storm has likely ruined the flintlocks.

KNOX

No doubt of that, sir—we'll have to use bayonets.

WASHINGTON

Order bayonets fixed, and the troops deployed ready to charge bayonets on command.

KNOX

Brigade, fix bayonets! (*voices repeat order, etc.*) Shall the artillery lead or follow, sir?

WASHINGTON

Follow and take position at the head of every street.

KNOX

Very good, sir.

WASHINGTON

Hm—two minutes—order the troops deployed.

KNOX

Deploy your troops—prepare to charge bayonets! (*command repeated—mob noise as order is obeyed*)

WASHINGTON

Keep your ears open for firing—it's nearly time. (*musketry*)

KNOX

There it is, sir!

WASHINGTON

Green has started! Order the charge, Knox! And God be with us!

KNOX

Forward! Charge bayonets! Ho! (*a great roar from the mob as the charge begins*)

ANNOUNCER

So Washington and his men swept into the village of Trenton, catching the Hessians totally unprepared! In an hour and a half it was all over.

The disposed army of ragamuffins put the Hessians to rout! It was the first great American victory of the Revolution, and its effect was enormous. The discouraged Colonists suddenly received new heart. Hope for the cause of independence had a rebirth, and Washington, instead of fighting a losing battle alone, found himself the leader of his countrymen in fact, as well as in name! In crossing the Delaware, Washington had saved the cause of American independence!

www.ingramcontent.com/pod-product-compliance
Lightning Source LLC
Chambersburg PA
CBHW032030040426
42448CB00006B/799